Do Not Bring Him Water
and other poems

℅

by Caitlin Scarano

Write Bloody Publishing
America's Independent Press

Los Angeles, CA

WRITEBLOODY.COM

Heidi,

Thank you so much for ~~joiny~~ joining us at Boneshaker. It was so great to meet you. I think we'd have a lot in common and hope we can stay in touch.
Let me know if you ever come to Washington!

Scarano, Caitlin.
1st edition.
ISBN: 978-1938912-78-8

Cover Designed by Zoe Norvell
Interior Layout by Winona Leon
Proofread by Lino Anunciacion
Edited by Jeanann Verlee

Type set in Bergamo from www.theleagueofmoveabletype.com

Printed in California, USA

Write Bloody Publishing
Los Angeles, CA

Support Independent Presses
writebloody.com

To contact the author, send an email to writebloody@gmail.com

MADE IN THE USA

For my father and the stories we did not get to tell each other.

DO NOT
BRING HIM
WATER

Do Not Bring Him Water

I.

II.

III.

I.

Underlying the whole long affair was a deep repetition compulsion, the term Freud used to describe the need to re-enact painful experiences in order to master them.

–Helen Macdonald, *H is for Hawk*

To the City with Her Skull Wind

A stray lamb. A blunt tire iron—weapon we are least bored of. Some days the sun howls over the lake. Some days I save snow crystals to prove to my tongue that they are not all unique. I move from room to room, mistake myself, my stale ribs, for someone else's house. Count your windows, city. The frost fingering every bashful crack. I've learned that all things leak—kitchen faucet with her pipes of marrow, teakettle, dog's eye, my mother's ivory pitcher filled with my father's black blood. Our human stained sheets. I keep a lover, city, but I dream of fucking animals and men who are faceless with hair, livers, feet. I don't dream of women anymore. I must believe I am still sensual. I must convince you of this. You know, last night he forced my throat over all of him with the back of his palm? It was the first time he ever did this. We came from mountains, animal fat, antler-handled blades. I had a vegetable garden, hens, a flock of white dogs. Now rock salt, parking tickets, this fear of being followed. During the night's bluest hour, your voice speaks to me, city, from the toilet bowl. You whisper, *No one is made for anyone.* Together, we hatch a baby bird paranoia. We chew his food, make him a nest of human hair. But I can't teach anything to fly. Not with these hands of spoiled milk and keratin. Count your windows, city. Watch how they erase me. As if I were a sentence, a woman.

Between the Bloodhounds and My Shrinking Mouth

There is artificial grass on the other side of this
electric fence,
                              her clicking tongue.

Of course, it's greener—greener than the emerald
eye you plucked from a sleeping man's
socket. Save it

for the licking hour. As a child, you don't ask
yourself why you're hiding,
                              you just hide.

I could be a specific story, the one
where he pretended to check me for a fever

        while I stood memorizing the horses
        in the fox hunt scenes of the wallpaper,
        the positions of their pulsing
        bodies, arc of their ankles,
        while I stood still as a snake counting
        the joints in my skull, imagining all
        I would swallow when I figured out how
        to uncoil myself and live the length
        of my body.

I could tell you this.

But my memory goes in and out like a car radio.

                    Self-indulgent girls—
just like those who eat

their scabs and only wash their hair
on Wednesdays—are not to be
encouraged.

                    What did I ask for?

I just wanted a velvet chair to crouch behind,
my grandmother's open dictionary
to masturbate to, and cold fried chicken

to split between the neighbor's bloodhounds
and my shrinking mouth.

I used to pinch my stomach skin
until it dazzled purple as an eggplant
again and again. Escalation

of the body's need.
I once bit my little sister's face to feel it.

                        I could not stop
laughing.

GOAT

In her vegetable garden, our mother grew more tomatoes than we or our neighbors could eat, so they rotted on the vine, little heads softened in the sun. My sisters and I hid under the benches of a gazebo our father built for her. We watched them. They were growing and building a home. Soon he would pin her to a red chair and then disappear in a mantle of moths. I would start stealing twenties from my grandmother's purse, and the boys at the bus stop would throw larger and larger rocks at my little sister's head.

But before all that, our parents bought us a baby goat, white as a dream, almost an offering. We called her Lacy and chained her to an apple tree near the gazebo. Whenever I touched her, she butted her head against my waist, gently at first but more aggressive as the summer wore on. I still remember the brutal rhythm of it. By fall she'd stripped the tree of all of its bark. We watched it die. We watched our mother trapped in the chair. We watched her scream on the end of her chain.

THE YELLOW BREAKDOWN

most people don't have signs and symptoms
in the early stages the liver is the second most
important organ in your body secretes bile for
the digestion of fats located under your rib cage
this includes a swollen tummy yellowish skin is
relatively rare making up around 1% of all weight
loss nausea water retention most children do not
have symptoms emesis (vomiting) nutrient-rich
blood is carried by the portal any doubt about the
place go somewhere else hepatocellular carcinoma
bilirubin yellow breakdown product of normal heme
catabolism enlarged breasts shrinking of testicles we
cannot survive regular high alcohol consumption
unprotected sex injecting drugs with shared needles
tend harmful substances in the blood not to be felt
or noticed until it is well advanced family history
people whose mother father brother or sister a
higher percentage of males bloating in the abdomen
water wells with arsenic spread to other parts of the
body the patient's health should not be significantly
undermined when trials reach the human stage they
are called clinical

WHAT YOU KILLED, WHAT YOU THOUGHT

I'm a drawn and quartered creature
curling around your feet. Useless

prey. *Yes*, you said, *I guess a part of me*
never wanted to be with you. Build the house,

hew the house. Can't glue together
the splinters of bedroom with come

and crushed cranberry. Your mind now—legless
animal. I look at photographs of us

by those bodies of water, your ripe mouth
frown-stained, as if I was fiddling with that grandfather

clock built into your chest. There was a time
when I knew you though—face, hands, pendulum.

Now I'm undressing with my winter teeth. Please
believe me: once, I glanced out

that kitchen window and saw our son
picking up sticks in a fragile coat. I never held

a trench knife behind my back, never
kept a poisonous lip up my flannel sleeve.

I was only mouthing mercy and an aggressive
thirst for you. The blue of my eye, you

could not name it. But I did not make it up.

What My Grandmother Didn't Say

Pray to the one who cuts you off at the knees.
The one who wicks you to a need.
I mistook the lion for a lark. Married
the schoolboy busy yanking other girls' braids.

In each generation a girl started to burn.
Witch child orbiting his dreams.
Schoolgirl tugging at the zipper
of his mouth. Unsealing a horror, our history.

Grandchild, you'll know him nightmare.
Feel him fingering the waistline of a doll.
His mouth soaked & sealed against your own.
No one will be allowed to speak.

He finger-folded daughters to paper dolls.
Tongue-traced granddaughters' tender jaws.
Your mother didn't speak to him, but wrote a letter
of blood pinched from her eyes. What never saw.

O, birdcage wire my jaw. Tongue black
while he dies under a church pew. Leave him there.
Forgive every daughter to pinch to pulp his eyes.
Cut him well above the knees. Pray for a son.

TOOLBOX

To my man in love
with state lines, end
rhymes, tobacco smoke sucked
through a cracked pickup truck window.

Footnote famous, crosses
stitched from shoelaces, that Florida
prison cell. Guitar wires
askew, wound and tightened,
askew.

The state he came to: Virginia,
magnolia tree. The open-mouth
lure of Tennessee: the state he left for.
Three daughters straddling
his best boots
so he shook them off.

Song of blue and red lights
against the rearview.
Psalm of Sunday, every shop
on Main Street empty. My starched
church dress. You, always
the itch against my nape.

Song to the southern
towns brimming with ghosts. To being
a ghost among ghosts, the clown
of ghosts, the last man explaining
love to a barstool.

To the closing hour. To the hammer
his father swung—so close
to sung—at his mother's skull.
To his roofing nails still embedded
in the hard of my heel. Those loose screws
beneath my teeth.

The toolbox he tucked behind
a row of damaged dolls. Rosary
pliers, crescent wrench.
To the liquid in the spirit
level.

DEAD DOG DONE

That old dog drug itself
across our autumn path, a man's
breath coating my face.
We've been looking for a dog, but not
a damaged dog, not a near-dead dog.
You can't fix the broken with a broken.

I'm running
down the ditch. Draping night
across my shoulders. I'm naked
except for the clothes and the cry.
Begging dog to look me in the eye. You
shameful, you turntail, matted surly.

When that dog dug itself out of our bed,
barked at the ghost of us.
What did you expect? Busy
turning keys between your teeth, purled
with burrow and maple and gleam.
No. I got real things to do, real shoes
to sew to real feet.

When that dog didn't drip or bowl,
why didn't you just leave me
on the nightroad   crawl and howl home?

THE ICE PICK BEING HER SHARPEST OBJECT

Shaded forever, the only way to be
hounded, by a man with buckshot

holes in the center of his chest.
Smoothbore arms flexing tattoos

like stains. His tobacco pipe-peppered
breath. Tapping

his foot from across the room.
My grandfather glued his shadow

over my bed with mucilage, a crushed
cream. Scarecrow effect,

to keep my girl body always
on edge. On my sixteenth birthday,

I chipped that scare-
crow down with my mother's ice pick.

Most of it came off in one rip, but some
strips still clung to the eaves. My mother

covered them with sun and moon
wallpaper. *Don't you come back*, I said

to the crow when I set it free
like the dog that bit the baby's face.

Maybe they are one and the same,
the crow and the dog. Maybe

a man is never an animal
and I've remembered it wrong.

But didn't antlers grow from his head
whenever my mother's back was turned?

Haven't I spent my whole life
recoiling?

THE WORD FOR IT

Does not come from *god*
or *ghost* or *dog*. Not even the ones
who bark at everything that moves.

Imagine us dancing at my winter
wedding. Bed sheets spun
with blood veins. His armless

chair. A mouth so muscled
he wore it. The threads of his
jaundiced jaw yellowing into

a rope bridge between my hands.
He didn't remember how to spell my name
but I memorized the corridors

and vampire mirrors of his.
The bottle's puppet, eyes
loose as marbles in a bone box.

The word doesn't root in *guardian*,
abuser, or *nauseated*, simply
originator of. Let me keep you

like snow in a tin
cup. We'll meet in a hospital
bed eleven years later.

Sickness, your hitching post.
Both of us refusing to play
the broken-necked horse.

Do Not Bring Him Water

If you go back, do not talk to the boy standing in the doorway. Leave him forever in the threshold. If you do talk to him, do not look him in the eyes. Don't compare the blue of them to your own (lighter, weaker). Do not attempt to make math or order out of two bodies that haven't even touched.

Do not drink so much that first night. Do not tell him you want him on the porch, the fall air cutting against your tongue. Don't offer him your last cigarette. Do not make him kiss you with his back against the wall or let him cry into your hands. Don't wake up the next day and notice how his stomach feels against your own. Instead, notice his hesitation, how his mouth pulls down at the corners in every photo you will take together. Do not mistake his beauty for capability.

That night in the rain, do not try to catch that stray, white dog on the side of the road. Do not see her face, her blind eyes pearled with cataracts. Don't desire a silence you will never be able to maintain. Do not ask him to help you. Do not even get out of the truck.

Don't fall in love with him under a blue owl right before the first snow that second September. Claim the hatchet he threw in the woods for fear of harming you and set out from that burning house. Keep your spine straight. Do not look back at how his knees buckle.

Know that you will always be hungry, that he will always leave you hungry. Know that he will mistake this hunger for anger and grow to fear you like a serpent wrapped around his bedpost. You will always be the one to do what needs to be done; the leaving will be no different. Do not meet his father. Do not come to love his mother. Know that there will be a day when their house will be as closed to you as the receding rooms of a dream. Know that there will be a day when you will never see them again.

Do not let him teach you anything: gentleness, how to shoulder a rifle, or how to start a fire in the woodstove. Do not make him meals night after night. Do not bring him water. Do not fold his clothes. Don't become the type of woman you will resent. Do not name your sons. Do not picture them in small coats battling with sticks in the yard.

Do not remember what he whispered as he came inside of you; instead, teach him to bury it. Do not accept his body as a burden for years. Recognize the weight of his arms across your chest; recognize the cage that you create. Do not be the monster. Do not be the apparition.

Do not try to make him your backcountry, your backstory. Listen to him when he speaks of winter and tells you that he does not dream: he is begging you to let him be. Don't touch the inside of his wrist. Take it back—your hand, your fingers. Remove them from his mouth. Do not write of the antlers you found in the birch grove. Do not think of their bodilessness, or who did the consuming. Do not name the animal you never saw.

Soap

because healing is slow

belly of blood
the body thy kingdom

come when he told me
he would wash
my mouth with a bar
of soap
I believed him

I licked a decorative seashell–
shaped soap to prepare myself
he would not be gentle
will be done
the inside
of my mouth would bruise
fruit that seemed okay to eat
on the outside

my mother prevented this
but what more is there than a human
touching another
our girl lives oscillated
around the prospect of his hands

skin's collision
my finger makes patterns
in your sweat on my summer
stomach

when my grandmother shot
her first buck did his belly
fill with blood under his guidance
our Father who art
she leads my mother
electrode silence padded
cell winter that drive to the abortion

clinic in Brooklyn how the shock
might have cradled her head
had it happened by God
the way you cradle mine

II.

A father, after all, is a lot for a thing to be.

–David Vann, *Legend of a Suicide*

The Barn You Used to Believe In

My father, my grandfathers: blue owls
with blue-black throats.

My muscular, spinespun birds,
sockets of black fluid, watching me
from the rafters.

Even when you're gone, I'll bone
hum. I'll pirouette for you.

Every bird in its boy has a cage.
Every girl comes from a procession—men,
ravens on a wire. Tin cans
on a log. Something waits

for us all—a blade beneath a sleeve
of skin, an aorta like a snake ready
to spring from tall grass, a black
cell that blooms
in the liver.

Death made them silent, mythology.
A hierarchy of animals
that I order and reorder.

Licking my hands
like a cat. Meticulous, obsessed
with what they did. What made me

sensual with shame: church
pew, barn, and batter bowl.

THE LAST TIME HE EVER TOUCHED ME

It was the end of a season. It was the end
of summer. We woke up beside each other
in a bed with white sheets. He touched me.
His mother was in the kitchen. She spoke
to the dog, her voice laughing
at the edges. She poured food in his metal
bowl. I spread my legs. The smell of coffee,
cinnamon. We were quiet, my mouth
was open. The sheets were flannel,
white. The door was ajar. A few inches.
She was in the kitchen. I could hear her
voice. My mouth was open for the last
time. I came. He touched me: white,
soft, metallic bowl. His mother's voice. Smell
of coffee and cinnamon. The end of a season.
I came, the door slightly open. My spine
white dog. Fingers that know her voice.
Metallic sound. His fingers spreading
four years. The door. The white dog covered
in a black sheet. Fingers that know my body's
seasons. Her voice my own. Curling spine,
arching for him. Did he know
it was the last time he would touch me,
my open voice curling, dissipating?
Did he imagine the sound of the next
season, the next man in whose hand
I would come? Come, the world is full
of bedrooms. Silhouette of leaves against
the streetlight and black sheets October
stiff. The first time always
carries the knowledge of the last: sleeping
little cell, secret half-life. Wind and rain
striking a window. My mouth slack, soft,
spreading. Him licking my spine, my exposed
neck. The door prying open at the edges
with laughter. The first time. I will be

nothing more than a neck for this one.
How they resist learning the body, following
its instructions like a dog. The last time,
last time, my little open. I was
the mother, a crack in the eyes of the door.
He was already gone, dissipating, sealing
the edges of my body, my neck, my little bird
in the hand of the next man.

MERELY BIRD AND BONNET

In my smallest room, a gold-green
finch afflicted with the voice
of a human infant. The smell
of nursery in reverse. The finch
suffocating on window
glass. What we let in
during the night: my little sister
killing things not to kill
herself. I will always think of her
without a daughter. The finch
and the robin. How she caught
them while the watching
world slept. What we do
not to kill, what we do not kill,
these are not the same. I refuse
to acknowledge her as a mother,
merely bird, merely bonnet.
We are still daughters. The robin's
body beaten into the nursery
rug. The finch on the windowsill
warm with its death. I will make her
monster, not mother (these are not
the same). Wake me with feathers
in my teeth. A gold-green smear
for a mouth. Ask me which one
of us collects baby bodies
in the night.

Her Father's House

self-born stench my mother as sacral as stretched

my mother as stuck between the walls of her

father's house at night I hear her crying

through the radiator vents I tap back a message *better you*

than me I guess and sleep with the head of a cat

under my pillow kitchen sweet I am eyeteeth deep

in paranoia

imagine my three-year-old niece finding a gun in her

shitty father's house and opening her face with it as women

we are hinge & boneink my grandmother's father was cold

to his daughters *distancing himself from them*

so that he would not molest them my aunt writes a man idles

his truck beside me as I jog up this fucking hill

slyribbed yes *she had it coming*

dressed like that in clothes and walking upright.

My Dangling Eyes

Last night, I pulled you
through the bowels of it.
Told you not to deny me.
Asked, where do you want me?
On top. I leaned back, bore
my fingers into the loam
of your abdomen.
Ghosts (I've named them: father,
grandfather) raking my hair.
Licking the lazurite stones
of my spine. You
said, Turn over. Like a fish,
like a man looking away,
like grace. You said
do this thing and I did. Open-
mouthed against the mattress,
slavering the winter
sheets. My dangling
eyes. I could not locate
your face for all the bedroom
dark. You were a cistern
of rainwater. I was a winding
staircase, newel & balustrade.
Smoothed and rounded
by you. When we came,
I cried blood. I tasted
rosehip. After, nothing
in this house
would meet my eye.

Night Mare

I'll conjure up a horse, a woman, succubus leech. Architecture
of sleep. Children under stress are more prone to night terrors.
The boa swallowing the baby. Her dozen, tire-thick spirals. *Marble-heavy,*
a bag full of God. My grandmother lured by confusion from room
to room, unable to recall what she lost. Her husband's body
beneath a morgue-white sheet, how I felt his skull turn toward
me even when I wasn't looking. The war he went to that he never
spoke of, the war inside of him that he never spoke of. The antlers
that grew from his head now sprout from my head. Screech owl.
Loose mare. The corners of the house, all her angles, twisted
like a net. A diseased mouth over my own. Was *mother*
the first word? Or was it *no*? My father with his steel-
toed boots. How we sat on his feet to prevent him from leaving.
Stomach in tangles. When we had food I couldn't eat. Pinching
the dog's neck until she cried out. *No one will know.*

ANIMAL TOOTH WET &

Animal tooth   wet &
loose   I learned the way
to water   by taking a hammer
to each kneecap   You were a boy
birch bent   broken swing chain
Stop me   if you've heard
this one   A summer
turtle shell of half   picked meat
The two men   who watched you
from their stopped car   the two men
who licked   that shell clean
How a human tongue   never
reminded you   of anything
You traded hipbones   for high
country   The book of nightmares
written by ankle   scabbed
children   you recognize
one of them as the boy   who hung
himself   from the magnolia
while you   chewed clover
and gave up   calling your mother
ma'am   threw her favorite
kitten in Crystal   Lake
like a lover   skipping
stones

THE EVENT HORIZON

X-rays of my grief show a dog, her legs
pierced with long screws. At first,
          we mistake the animal

for a human with a tapered tail. We can't decide
if the screws are torturous or surgical.
          So we leave

the images silhouetted against the window,
pack a picnic, and go down to the river.
          Every betrayal

begins in a small intimacy—measuring
your teeth against my teeth. Watching
          the hairline crack

in the plaster above our bed for a drop of blood
or an invitation. There is a man behind me.
          He fell through

the ceiling glass. Don't you see him? He's crawled
after me since I was robin's egg
          blue, nothing but a girl. Patient, he

will outlast you. The black hole
in my dreaming
          will outlast you.

Coming To

Chin resting on the edge of a toilet bowl, strings
of vomit branching from my mouth; in the middle
of a street corner screaming match
with a lover I am about to lose; coming to
as he discovers the kitchen knife I hid under the nightstand;
just as my hair catches on fire; pissing
in the snow in a birchgrove, in the distance I hear a girl
call my name and it sounds
simultaneously like a warning & a threat;
coming to as the taxi driver asks *how much*
for me to fuck him; lost in a city that isn't mine,
a narrative that isn't mine; in a field
just as it catches on fire; coming to
with a fistful of glass; as I scratch my face open
with my fingernails; begging *just sleep beside me*
this one night; begging
help me please but he won't
get out of the truck; coming to
on the other side of a mirror beside a living
room hospice bed.

In this dream, I am surrounded by buckets of blood and they are all
different shades. Infinite variations within one thing.

Listen: I am good at being a drunk because I am skilled at shame.

My persona here revolves around it.
I will answer to any night-soaked desperation you offer.

I am in a corner surrounded by buckets of blood
and yes, this is a metaphor but it is true
that I cannot leave
without spilling some of them.

ENGRAVING

Carve your name into his back
like quivering tree
bark. After, exhausted by the act,

your wrist pulsing like a little clock,
fingers curved about the helve, fall
asleep by the trunk. Wet

leaves between you and the worms.
Wake up surprised to find the pocketknife
in your hand, the tip of it

still bloody. Test your pointer finger against it.
Feel it stick for just a moment.
Taste your finger as if you've done this

gesture thousands of times. Move toward the false
laughter of water, that fishing line hooked
in your belly. When it tugs, gag

from the back of your throat—
the black boot of the man you swallowed still
kicking. Wash the knife in the water until it grins,

all high sun and silver. They will come
searching in the night, lantern light
bouncing off the boulders like bodies.

Do not fight when they find you.
Keep your canine teeth from clicking. Dazzle them
with one of your many faces. Hide the knife

back in a pocket of skin.
When they threaten to throw you
in the lake, when they bind

your wrists and ankles together, let them name you
witch. Don't admit anything
to the chorus of bleeding trees.

                                  The forest will find its own fool to blame.

SCATTER

Begin with a man match that grows into a girl
when struck. Oval flame. Face like her father's
with eyes that do not startle. A seething

center, blue-hot as the self I found
beneath the surface when I shed my skin
that nineteenth year.

> When I said *I will have no more*
> *of this*: dreams of my grandfather touching
> my mother in a secret room behind
> the radiator grate.

I stripped off that stained
dress and began a bestiary.

Not every snakehead
was a man's fist needing to be
severed from its neck.

Not every finger
will be unwanted.

But a worm moon swells
in the corner of my bed, and I love the smell
of a nightmare coming on. A boy who knows when
to press the giving walls
of my throat. I still hear the howling
house, remember the baby
dolls my grandmother hid beneath the steps.

> It was from that back porch that I threw
> his favorite cat just to see
> how she would land. Afterward, he twisted
> my elbow behind my body and brought
> his teeth next to my ear.

I don't remember what he whispered
but when I was twelve his aorta
crawled from his chest as if summoned.
The rope was finally freed
from the well of bowered water,
the bone bucket left to sink.

The years of the next decade scatter
like my mother's hens when the neighbor's dog
got loose and killed as many as it could
before they hid on top of the coop.

    I still picture her standing in the aftermath,
    picking up bloody feathers as if
    she's collecting talismans.

LOCKED

Stand in the middle of winter and speak of summer,
your mouth fragile & green.

Every devotion is a twisted rope with two ends.
Think of a burial. How close that word is to *boy*.

Think of the feverdream as a harvest, the room
spinning even and low as a record.

Or that time you saw two bull moose
antlerlocked in a clearing, snow just starting to fall.

Every aggression is instinctual. Picture the pockets
in your body. How much time you wasted

imagining sons with boneweak men. Last
night you dreamt that your mother was dead

and you inherited her house. All of that softened
glass suddenly yours.

POOL

my father knew a guy
with an inground pool the walls
and bottom of which were painted midnight
blue summers he took us there
so we could learn to tire our own bodies
while he popped open silver cans
and laughed from cement sidelines
until the year he receded like a rearview town
that shrinks and shrinks until
it is nothing but a speck I never felt okay
I couldn't see the floor couldn't see
myself how far down his death
two decades later would be how bottomless
it felt like I was diving
into an inky lagoon or a black hole
the years that would darken between us
like a blotted-out constellation or his mother's eyes
swollen shut after I sat on the hardwood
floor of my apartment reading cards
he sent that I never responded to *Would love
to talk with you, call me sometime* look at me
now strong swimmer laughing
at the men on the sidelines that summer
he was always there smiling
at me but his gaze was just over my right
shoulder sizing up the escape route
that would end in a 100 pound body
jaundiced lymph node rotted
pinholed pupils fluid filled abdomen how hard
it is to recognize someone
even when you think you have them

History of Blue

when I think of her I see a wooden spoon and a white bowl
        I see a kitchen with a daughter kneading dough
    she is laughing
we are laughing
        when I drove through the desert I thought of him
    when I was lost in a bruised valley I thought of him
when a boy held me as I told him I didn't love him
        I thought and I thought until the world fell away
    exoskeleton after exoskeleton
until nothing was left but me in this room
        I could touch each corner and remember a lover
    myself crying on the floor
I still don't know why I do what I do
        for this I certainly understand your anger
    the pitch of it richer than your morality
she taught me how to bake bread
        but I remember nothing
    she taught me to soften
but I remember nothing
        a man can be full of stories guitar wires a bloated heart
    he can be all this and still have a fist or two
but what does it matter
        for how the song was wasted
    after all that no one cares if you get sober or clean
they just care how you dance for them
        how you (un)dress and dilate your ruin
    in shades of streetlamp and sidewalk glass
we can love what harms us
        mourn what harmed us
    the key would not turn in the hole
it was made for
        he kicked in the back door
    a house a yard of unfinished projects
the arbor unarched the bedroom closets undoored
        after he left this history of blue
    spindrift three daughters unanchored we flew

through trees we saw ghosts in off-white suits
            we tasted the garden for its graves
      in every season we bleed we breathe
we bolt
            unweapon the want
      fucking almost a form
of healing unbraid my hair
            bring me water not pity
      for how the song was wasted

III.

most things in nature have no meaning

–Beth Bachmann, *Do Not Rise*

The Boar I Bled

During the rawest year, I live inside the ribcage of an elk, eat
fish from a jar and drink stale snow I saved

from the winter before. I don't make notches
in trees. I do not believe the moon follows me. In the fall, a boy

rides by on his best stick horse. He's coming from a war and has white
knight inclinations, but I smell

of wood smoke and lye and don't even own an ivory dress. I do not
braid my hair or sing to misty-eyed animals at the window.

I don't even have a window.

I drained the gentleness from myself as if bleeding a boar.
Instead of saving each other, me and the boy get drunk

on sour dandelion wine and stories of our fathers. We marvel
at sounds, but rarely speak a common language.

When the fire lowers to nothing but embers, he whistles,
then he, the night, and the bodiless horse are gone. I count

the places he found on me, my body smoldering, my hunger
renewed and thrashing.

In the morning, I try turning myself inside out,
but he hasn't left any grape seeds or sons behind. Listen:

you don't need something to remember someone by. The sky can cut
open her own underbelly and snow will follow.

For the Occasion

An all-black wasp.

My spine
wrung bell.

I beg you.

Eyes nuclear
winter blue.

Do you still dream
in marrow, funeral
precision?

My all-black
wasp eating my all-
black moth. Silky
with blood.

I wore my grandfather's
human-hair wig
for the occasion.

Applied fake eye-
lashes. You refuse to
imagine, so I will.

I can't name the master.
I cannot recognize
this room for a house.

Girls with chandelier
faces. Is there a bone
that most resembles you?

I lit the wig on fire.
Threw it in the toilet
bowl's pristine water.

That night, your face
smelt of spoiled milk.

I was a child counting
her ribs, eating her
scabs. Lust,

a black wasp
waiting
on her pillow.

BLACK HOLE IN A JAR

night grow me more
teeth this doll was made
with a mouth that doesn't open
though the girl presses
a plastic bottle
hard to its face
the child who wants
a child my mother hallowed
searching a garden for her
lost engagement diamond
the black hole marriage
the field from which nothing can escape
no. night grow me more teeth
more tongue she got out
through a crack
beneath the door
she got out from the radiator
vent where he caged her in my dreams
there is a daughter every
opening in her a black hole
my niece drags her dolls
by their wrists across
the kitchen floor she is
not a garden not a test
not a metaphor she is lucky
to be alive after her father
choked my sister on a mattress
when she was pregnant
as children we caught
fireflies in a jar
which smelled both stale
and sweet in the morning
after they'd died my mother
dumped them in the grass
said *this is not a lesson*

ON HAVING A DAUGHTER, RELUCTANT

It's like trying to gather an echo with just your hands
and a bit of honey. Trying to walk the fence

line at night with only oxblood marbles
for eyes. Would you rather create a thing

that will dominate or one that will be dominated?
Let me be my own commandments. Let me fuck myself

to motherhood as if it were a pinnacle or an orbit.
Woman is not *vessel.*

I've stood on both sides of this country
ankle-deep in salt water and the sound

of my own blood. I do not want to give birth to myself.
I want to be my arsonist, to set fire

to my own house. I will not love or hate my body.
I said, I will not love or hate my body.

MULE

His coffin and the petals
of an opening mouth.
He was an absence,
a complete absorption of light.

Tongue rot, funeral rot—
these are not the same.

Master made by hound. Man
and the dog he drags
by an invisible length of rope.
Shepherd, give me back
my country of winter.
Give me back silence

between bleached streets. Moon
resting her belly on the tin roof
of a farmhouse. Mother hiding
sounds of sobbing behind a marble-
handled door. The creatures of her own

father's hands. The warm eggs
I found between the bricks
near the coop, how sometimes
the harder surfaces are where
we need to nest.

Mule I made from pillow innards,
chicken wire, and the leather
of a lampshade. The difference
between infertility and impotency.

We all had a choice.

I set fire to the Virginia field and rode
out. Made for a mountain, her
crown of snow. A single
spider crossed my cheek.

How I untangled
the fishing wire from flesh.
How I learned to unlove that man
before I swallowed the hook
of his death.

ANNOTATION

During the season of still water, I take a lamp down from the sky
and cross a midwestern field. It is winter but there is no snow.

If I am here, it means I am looking for something. Maybe you.
Or the spot where I buried the crescent wrench

with her adjustable jaw. She would not stop confessing. I put her
in the hole beside his claw hammer. I imagine

they tell each other stories without morals and *walked into a bar*
jokes all night. Every storm is surreal when you realize the world

is not for you. No, I mean that the world goes on with
or without you. I take a lamp down. I step into a clearing.

Wind scrapes my face to its most basic form: a man's
footprints frozen in the mud.

LITTLE SPINES

I promise you this mouth of snake
    smoke,
      summer like a gutted country

church house: field rich,
    steeple stunted,
      overgrown with fireweed, pews

broken & picked like teeth. The stained
    glass in your eyes
      saggy,

distorted by a grinning
    gravity. I abrade
      my knuckles on the red

brick walls of you—what will be
    long left standing.
      Where men

sleep beneath the floor.
    I promise you this splayed
      watchdog. No need

for a chain
    chewed bedpost.
      No need

for ticking, the pull of blood
    like needle-loyal thread
      through your body.

We start at the end. I promise
    you cradles.
      I promise you coffins.

When we were in the forest of legs,
    when we were children with different
    connotations for wolves,

each finger was a little spine,
    unbroken and accusing. Every time
    we fucked we made an alcove

in the garden. A hedge maze designed
    with no way out. Brother, blood still
    lines my fingernails. I still sleep

under a mobile of tire irons.
    Oh holy night.
    Oh how they ring.

Rabbit Holes

How strange to live in a lived-in space. To speak
for the dead, to carry the heart

of a blue owl. I was in love
before I met you. Before I met anyone, I was folding

towels in my mother's dining room and I swear
all the angles of the house pointed at me

and then pointed the way out. Busy mending
my mind of barking dogs.

I know now I wasn't afraid of mirrors
because I thought I might tip into them. It was my reflection

I was avoiding. The rabbit hole that is my face. The church
pew I hid beneath taught me

to keep still. Disciplined as the man in the alley flashing
his loneliness from under an army

coat. That was the year a girl died in the house next door
to my grandparents'. She was so blonde and the blue

rings underneath her eyes I thought I could kiss like a pool
of water and dive into. He held my mouth

over the doorknob. Whispered, *Teach me
such loveliness.*

Questions I Never Asked Him

Why did you pretend not to notice the way your father spoke to your
mother?

> I'm sorry. I know you always wanted me
> to be noble. But, unlike you, I didn't have years of practice kissing
> stove coils and sweeping cottonmouths from the doorstep.

When I stood on the side of the road and begged for you to help me,
what did you whisper to the rain?

> I said *I want it back*—my birch grove boyhood,
> the hair you shaved from your head that second year, the last
> coyote I shot beneath the cottonwoods.

If you could have been any other animal, which would it have been?

> You, mixing flour and water in a white bowl
> with a wooden spoon while the neighbor's huskies
> howled at the unseen.

Do you remember the last thing I whispered in my sleep?

> *Each morning, I sit by this window of snow*
> *you surrendered and try on sentences like faces.*

Why did you blame me for the teeth you swallowed?

> Wasn't I with you when your father died?
> Didn't you stir the dark lake in me for its creatures?

Yes, but who will I be now?

> Burn an acre behind the house. Tend the edges
> of that fire until fall.

When did you realize we would not have children? Did you feel a loss
then?

It must have been when I found the severed
head of a cat, still blinking, in our bed.
I don't know about loss,
but I paused before burying it
toddler-deep.

Reenactment

Two howls lay beside each other
in a batter bed. From the same garden,

but not the same stem. I imagine
my mother drowning

suitcases full of his photos
in a river of milk,

silt, and snake skin. (After death,
the living reenact the event

until sensual, blunted.) Fine. Take
some of the magic out of it,

but the space will blossom
with its own dark matter.

I try to vomit behind the arbor
he built for her but nothing surfaces.

Why not eat the image or use it
to start a fire that will swallow

the house? A yellow-skulled bird
in love with the window's warp,

a distorted family of faces.
I can look no more

or less like him
now.

PRAISE

"Tell me about it if it's something human. Let me into your grief."
    –Robert Frost

to the rocking chair my maternal grandmother
lurches breastfeeding porcelain dolls. To her
husband's collection of tobacco pipes, polished
smooth as his tongue. Praise to such a forked
man. Living within the walls of their angers,
I blossomed. My mother, coral canary
on the shoulder of longhaired men. My older
sister kissing the swastika tattoo on a sallow
boy's bicep, beautifully bent as she scoops
up her belongings from the snow year after year.
On our family's kitchen table, my little sister
crushed cochineals. Every lover she dyed
a rattled carmine until the man that cracked
her womb like a tumid pecan. Now she wields
a cast-iron skillet over his head: *You better kill me*
before I kill you. I know no metaphor to protect
or alter. An ashtray swiping a freckled forehead,
a hammer opening my paternal grandmother's skull
like sunlight on a peony
                          pulsing with ants.

After Living in You Long Enough

like a house like a season I would know
when the leaving was welling up
depression wringing and ringing your body
to a limp rag ineffectual ravens laughing
at each other across our yard of snow
I thought we might make it if I was good
if you were good if you were like a house
full of glass hours full of ribbon
black ravens full of your mother's best
versions of you women who have only sons
women who have only daughters bent
like wire hangers for some purpose
be useful be house hard like glass
not shatterable never break never bleed
never be a person on your knees
be better just a bit more patient depthless
as a well give and give and let him drink
of you *love him as he is* they said serotonin
spilt like sugar I swept through the cracks
my anger wringing him out limping
through the woods to find the hatchet
he hid from himself I was never patient
enough never enough I could not be
his best season only ribbon black anger
the son we didn't have but swear I saw playing
in the snow of the yard I shared with the boy
who was good but *not stable* he said *I am not
stable* and I thought of a mare starving
shatterable loose the time we saw those wild
horses on the side of the road in the Yukon
Territory neither of us could believe it
they were there they were there

they were right in front of you

PARTINGS

Sever the night cloak latched
        around your neck.

Take my father's hands that clutch the claw
        hammer.

Sever the grief,
        sever the hammer.

Remove the skin from my face
        so I will stop mistaking myself

for my mask. Sever my vanity.
        Gather the wolves in the silo.

The imagined family
        farm now abandoned. Let their howls

become cylindrical, taut. You may sever
        the barn with fire,

but these bastard bones
        should stay in our bodies.

Call out your demons
        for their long-limbed indifference.

I am more than a bedpost, more than
        what keeps me tied to it.

I am the exposed parts
        of a watch face, the ticking

beneath a tongue I haven't touched
        with my own. Driftless

the body in the skull's
        canal. I came

to a point in my life that I could not sustain.
      Suffer the creature,

sever the soil from this eave of roots. Forget
      our lover looking back at you

from a field of snow struck blue
      by the fists of an orbiting

moon. There are rooms of silver,
      winter. Sugar

separated from the blood.
      There were whole days

when I didn't speak. Now, detritus
      in and out of my mouth, smell

of wormwood, this black wasp
      between my sheets. Separate her

wings from the thorax
      for she is curious.

Marvel at her exoskeleton's
      slender waist.

Marvel, too, an act of severance.
      We no longer bow

beside our beds at night. I am no longer afraid
      of fucking strangers

or being caught under a streetlight
      as it flickers out. Fear

is a form of separation. I've carved a hole
      into my palm. Let's watch the light

pass through. Gender now
      uninteresting. A dog whistles back

                    at the shadow calling to it.

Acknowledgements

Deep gratitude to my friends and faculty at the University of Alaska Fairbanks and the University of Wisconsin-Milwaukee.

Thanks to the Write Bloody family!

SB, thank you for all the adventures and your constant support of my work.

Thank you to my family for allowing me to tell our stories.

Sue Scarano, thank you most of all.

I am extremely grateful to the following publications where versions of these poems first appeared:

Beecher's Magazine: "Her Father's House"

Bellingham Review: "For the Occasion"

Best New Poets 2016: "Mule"

Colorado Review: "Merely Bird and Bonnet"

concīs: "Locked"

Five Quarterly: "Little Spines"

Fugue: "Partings" and "Dead Dog Done"

Ghost Proposal: "Black Hole in a Jar"

Ghost Town: "What You Killed, What You Thought"

Granta: "Night Mare" and "The Ice Pick Being Her Sharpest Object"

Hobart: "Pool" and "Goat"

Indiana Review: "Between the Bloodhounds and My Shrinking Mouth" and "To the City with Her Skull Wind"

Ninth Letter: "Scatter"

Poetry Northwest: "Annotation"

Poet's Billow: "Praise," "My Dangling Eyes," and "What My
  Grandmother Didn't Say"

Poor Claudia: Crush: "Soap"

Radar Poetry: "Mule"

Room Magazine: "Reenactment"

So to Speak: "Toolbox"

The Puritan: "The Last Time He Ever Touched Me"

The Thought Erotic: "Questions I Never Asked Him"

Wildness: "The Boar I Bled"

Word Riot: "Animal Tooth Wet &"

Yemassee: "Rabbit Holes"

ABOUT THE AUTHOR

Photo by Jithu Ramesh

Caitlin Scarano is currently a doctoral candidate in English with a concentration in Creative Writing at the University of Wisconsin-Milwaukee. She was born in Florida, but raised in rural Virginia. She has an MA in College Student Personnel from Bowling Green State University and an MFA in Poetry from the University of Alaska Fairbanks. Her poem "Mule" was selected for the *Best New Poets 2016* anthology, and her flash fiction piece "Pitcher of Cream" was included in *The Best Small Fictions 2016*. She has two poetry chapbooks: *The White Dog Year* (dancing girl press, 2015) and *The Salt and Shadow Coiled* (Zoo Cake Press, 2015). For more, see caitlinscarano.com

IF YOU LIKE CAITLIN SCARANO,
CAITLIN SCARANO LIKES...

Floating, Brilliant, Gone
Franny Choi

The Pocketknife Bible
Anis Mojgani

Said The Manic To The Muse
Jeanann Verlee

Pecking Order
Nicole Homer

Write Bloody Publishing distributes and promotes great books of fiction, poetry and art every year. We are an independent press dedicated to quality literature and book design, with an office in Austin, TX.

Our employees are authors and artists so we call ourselves a family. Our design team comes from all over America: modern painters, photographers and rock album designers create book covers we're proud to be judged by.

We publish and promote 8-12 tour-savvy authors per year. We are grass-roots, D.I.Y., bootstrap believers. Pull up a good book and join the family. Support independent authors, artists and presses.

**Want to know more about Write Bloody books, authors and events?
Join our maling list at**

www.writebloody.com

WRITE BLOODY BOOKS

CPSIA information can be obtained
at www.ICGtesting.com
Printed in the USA
FSOW01n2103150917
38713FS